The Don't Laugh Challenge™

6 YEAR OLD EDITION

Don't Laugh Challenge
BONUS PLAY

Join our Joke Club and get the Bonus Play PDF!

★★★★★★★★★★★★★★

Simply send us an email to:

➤ **bacchuspublish@gmail.com** ◀

and you will get the following:

• 10 BONUS hilarious jokes!

• An entry in our Monthly Giveaway of a
$25 Amazon Gift card!

We draw a new winner each month and will contact you via email!
Good luck!

Welcome to
The Don't Laugh Challenge ™

• How do you play?

The Don't Laugh Challenge is made up of 10 rounds with 2 games in each round. It is a 2-3 player game with the players being 'Jester #1','Jester #2', and a 'King' or 'Queen'. In each game you have an opportunity to score points by making the other players laugh.

After completing each round, tally up the points to determine the Round Champion! Add all 10 rounds together to see who is the Ultimate Don't Laugh Challenge Master! If you end up in a tie, use our final Tie Breaker Round for a Winner Takes All!

• Who can play the game?

Get the whole family involved! Grab a family member or a friend and take turns going back and forth. We've also added Bonus Points in game 2, so grab a 3rd person, a.k.a 'King' or 'Queen', and earn an extra point by making them guess your scene!

The Don't Laugh Challenge™
Activity Rules

- ## Game 1 - Jokes (1 point each)

  Jester #1 will hold the book and read each joke to Jester #2. If the joke makes Jester #2 laugh, Jester #1 can record a point for the joke. Each joke is worth 1 point. At the end of the jokes, tally up your total Joke Points scored for Jester #1 and continue to Game 2!

- ## Game 2 - Silly Scenarios (2 points each + bonus point)

  Without telling the other Jester what the scenarios say, read each scenario to yourself and then get creative by acting it out! You can use sound effects, but be sure not to say any words! If you make the other Jester laugh, record your points and continue to the next scenario.

  BONUS POINT: Get your parents or a third player, a.k.a King or Queen, involved and have them guess what in the world you are doing! Get the King or Queen to guess the scene correctly and you score a BONUS POINT!

The Don't Laugh Challenge ™
Activity Rules

Once Jester #1 completes both games it is Jester #2's turn. The directions at the bottom of the book will tell you who goes next. Once you have both completed all the games in the round, add your total points from each game to the Round Score Page and record the Round winner!

• How do you get started?

Flip a coin. If guessed correctly, then that Jester begins!

Tip: Make any of the activities extra funny by using facial expressions, funny voices or silly movements!

Jokes

Where does the cat keep her money?

In her PURR-se!

___/1

What do dogs eat at the movies?

PUP-corn!

___/1

What did the cheddar say when they took his picture?

"Cheese!"

___/1

Why didn't the Scarecrow want a second helping?

He was stuffed!

___/1

JOKES TOTAL: ___/4

JESTER 1 CONTINUE TO THE NEXT PAGE ➡

Silly Scenarios

(Act it out!)

You are a giant, terrifying T-Rex with tiny arms and a very itchy back! Get creative and show how you would scratch that itch that you can't reach!

_____ /2

You are a happy little puppy running around the yard and playing, when the floor suddenly turns to a bouncy trampoline! Woah!!

_____ /2

SILLY SCENARIOS TOTAL: _____ /4

NOW, PASS THE BOOK TO JESTER 2 ➡

Jokes

JESTER 2

What do weightlifters and toddlers have in common?

Pull-ups!   /1

Why did the T-Rex fail gym class?

He couldn't touch his toes.   /1

What does the chalk enjoy on cold winter nights?

Hot CHALK-late!   /1

What toothpaste flavor do dogs love most?

PUP-permint!   /1

JOKES TOTAL: _____ /4

Silly Scenarios

(Act it out!)

There's a happy family of frogs hopping around and licking up flies. Pretend to be one of the frogs and partake in the fun!

_____ /2

Pretend to be a cuckoo clock and move your hands while using sounds. When your hands hit the hour, show your best cuckoo clock impression!

_____ /2

SILLY SCENARIOS TOTAL: _____ /4

TiME TO SCORE YOUR POiNTS! ➔

JESTER 1

/8

ROUND TOTAL

JESTER 2

/8

ROUND TOTAL

ROUND
CHAMPION

Jokes

What's inside a ghost's nose?

BOO-gers!

_____ /1

Who ate all the pastries in the kitchen?

I **DONUT** know!

_____ /1

Why did the cow want to be alone?

It was in a bad **MOOOO**-d!

_____ /1

What kind of diamond is huge, but never sparkles?

A baseball diamond.

_____ /1

JOKES TOTAL: _____ /4

Silly Scenarios

(Act it out!)

Pretend to ride a horse with your eyes closed
- **NO PEEKING!** Until you hit a bump and
pretend to almost fly off!

/2

You are pretending to practice sword
fighting by yourself. You watch it fly into the
air and land into the ground. You try pulling it
out, but only to slip back and fall!

/2

SILLY SCENARIOS TOTAL: /4

NOW, PASS THE BOOK TO JESTER 2 ➜

Jokes

JESTER 2

Why did the pig blow his nose?

He had a ham-BOOGER!

/1

Why did everyone love the tortoise?

He was TURTLE-y awesome!

/1

What kind of food is a genius' favorite?

BRAIN food!

/1

What is a duck's favorite snack?

Cheese and QUACKers!

/1

JOKES TOTAL: _____ /4

JESTER 2 CONTINUE TO THE NEXT PAGE ➜

Silly Scenarios

(Act it out!)

Build an imaginary snowman. Roll, stack, and decorate your snowman - but don't forget to show how cold you are!

/2

You're a beautiful ballerina dancing and spinning around. Mop the floor while you dance and try to keep your balance!

/2

SILLY SCENARIOS TOTAL: _____ /4

TiME TO SCORE YOUR POINTS! ➔

JESTER 1

/8

ROUND TOTAL

JESTER 2

/8

ROUND TOTAL

ROUND
CHAMPION

Jokes

What is a policeman's favorite board game?

Mo-COP-oly! (Monopoly)

/1

What footwear is made from banana peels?

SLIP-pers!

/1

What kind of sea creature loves to perform?

The Starfish!

/1

Where do veggies like to eat dinner?

In their mush-ROOM!

/1

JOKES TOTAL: /4

JESTER 1 CONTINUE TO THE NEXT PAGE →

Silly Scenarios

(Act it out!)

Act like a T-rex playing mini-golf! Show how a T-Rex celebrates when he makes a hole-in-one!

/2

You are a cat that just woke up from a nap. Stretch like a cat by putting your butt in the air and letting out a big yawn!

/2

SILLY SCENARIOS TOTAL: _____ /4

 NOW, PASS THE BOOK TO JESTER 2 ➡

Jokes

What do you call a good looking pickle?

A CUTE-cumber!

/1

Where do the school of fish go when they don't feel well?

To the Nurse Shark!

/1

What do dogs like even more than pancakes?

Woofles! (Waffles)

/1

What is the Xbox's favorite bathroom game?

/1

Call of Doodie!

JOKES TOTAL: _____ /4

Silly Scenarios

(Act it out!)

You bend over to pick something up and pretend to feel somebody tap you from behind, but when you look back... there's nothing there. **SPOOKY!**

/2

An ambulance got hurt! What kind of sound would a siren in pain make? Show the crowd!

/2

SILLY SCENARIOS TOTAL: _____ /4

TIME TO SCORE YOUR POINTS! ➡

JESTER 1

/8

ROUND TOTAL

JESTER 2

/8

ROUND TOTAL

ROUND
CHAMPION

ROUND
4

Jokes

What do you call a sandwich at a school?

A SUB-stitute teacher!

_____ /1

What subject do snakes like?

HISS-tory!

_____ /1

What movie do Santa's elves love the most?

A Toy Story.

_____ /1

What did the angry cat say to his little babies?

"Are you kitten me?"

_____ /1

JOKES TOTAL: _____ /4

JESTER 1 CONTINUE TO THE NEXT PAGE ➜

Silly Scenarios

(Act it out!)

You're a turtle who is stuck on your back. Try everything you can think of to flip back over onto your feet! It's tough being a turtle!

/2

Act like a goofy kangaroo that is doing the chicken dance. Make sure that you hop a lot!

/2

SILLY SCENARIOS TOTAL: _____ /4

 NOW, PASS THE BOOK TO JESTER 2 ➡

Jokes

Why did the kids get sent to the stable?

For horsing around!

/1

What's black, white, and brown all over?

A dalmatian rolling in the mud!

/1

How can you tell when a pig farts?

It smells like bacon!

/1

What do you call a rabbit that tells jokes?

A funny bunny!

/1

JOKES TOTAL: _____ /4

Silly Scenarios

(Act it out!)

Act out the song, "Head, shoulders, knees, and toes!" as if you were a long-necked giraffe.

_____ /2

Act like a desperate fish out of the water, gasping for air! Flop all over until you get yourself back into the ocean!

_____ /2

SILLY SCENARIOS TOTAL: _____ /4

TIME TO SCORE YOUR POINTS! ➜

JESTER 1

/8

ROUND TOTAL

JESTER 2

/8

ROUND TOTAL

ROUND CHAMPION

ROUND 5

Jokes

What ballet play do the ducks perform every Christmas?

The Nut-QUACKER!

/1

Why did the leopard wear the same thing every day?

A leopard can't change its spots!

/1

What is peanut butter's favorite type of fish?

The JELLY-fish!

/1

What candy loves the playground?

Recess Pieces!

/1

JOKES TOTAL: ____ /4

JESTER 1 CONTINUE TO THE NEXT PAGE ➜

Silly Scenarios

(Act it out!)

You're not supposed to be sleeping, but you're so tired. Every time you fall asleep, jolt yourself awake and look around confused!

/2

Suddenly, your body becomes Jell-O and you can't stop wiggling! Woah!!!

/2

SILLY SCENARIOS TOTAL: _____ /4

NOW, PASS THE BOOK TO JESTER 2 ➡

Jokes

What do you call a nosey dog?

Snoopy.

/1

What do you call a lion at the Zoo?

The mane attraction!

/1

How does a mermaid make calls?

With her SHELL-phone!

/1

Why did the ocean go to the ball game?

To do the wave!

/1

JOKES TOTAL: _____ /4

Silly Scenarios

(Act it out!)

You're a wild chimpanzee running back and forth inside of your cage. You should also try breaking out! (Tip: Don't forget your monkey sounds!)

/2

You are a cowboy in the Wild West, riding your horse in a high-speed chase around the room! Keep riding and let out a little "Yippie Ki-Yay!"

/2

SILLY SCENARIOS TOTAL: _____ /4

TiME TO SCORE YOUR POINTS! ➔

JESTER 1

/8

ROUND TOTAL

JESTER 2

/8

ROUND TOTAL

ROUND
CHAMPION

ROUND

6

Jokes

What do you call it when your sandwich and chips fight?

Lunch BOX-ing!

/1

Who is a cat's favorite musician?

Kitty Perry!

/1

What did the shovel say to the ground?

"I really dig you!"

/1

Why can't you tell a secret to snakes?

Because they're RATTLE-tales!

/1

JOKES TOTAL: _____ /4

JESTER 1 CONTINUE TO THE NEXT PAGE →

Silly Scenarios

(Act it out!)

You are a giant robot who loves to dance, and your favorite song just came on! Show how robots get down!

/2

Pretend to open your door and greet your puppy! Don't forget to show how excited you are!

/2

SILLY SCENARIOS TOTAL: _____ /4

NOW, PASS THE BOOK TO JESTER 2 ➜

43

Jokes

What's the quietest part of a computer?

The mouse!

/1

What is an elf's favorite type of car?

TOY-ota!

/1

How did the turtle become less shy?

It came out of its shell!

/1

What do you call an alligator that can't stand up straight?

A CROOKED-ile!

/1

JOKES TOTAL: _____ /4

JESTER 2 CONTINUE TO THE NEXT PAGE ➜

Silly Scenarios

(Act it out!)

There are ants in your shoes! Dance like a crazy person while flailing your feet around to try and get rid of them in any way possible!

/2

You are a little piglet running around (Use 'Oink' noises). You see a puddle of mud and squeal in excitement! Run, jump, and roll in the mud while oinking in happiness!

/2

SILLY SCENARIOS TOTAL: _____ /4

TIME TO SCORE YOUR POINTS! ➔

JESTER 1

/8

ROUND TOTAL

JESTER 2

/8

ROUND TOTAL

ROUND
CHAMPION

Jokes

What's a baby ghost's favorite game?

Peek-a-BOO!

_____ /1

Did you hear the cashew and almond started dating?

They're NUTS about each other!

_____ /1

What do you call an ape that's good at soccer?

A GOAL-rilla!

_____ /1

Where does Wonder Woman do her shopping?

The SUPER-market.

_____ /1

JOKES TOTAL: _____ /4

JESTER 1 CONTINUE TO THE NEXT PAGE ➡

Silly Scenarios

(Act it out!)

Drop down on all fours and become a cow who loves to moo loudly, while doing your favorite dance moves!

/2

You're an elephant with a runny nose. Use your arm as a trunk while you sneeze and blow it, loudly!

/2

SILLY SCENARIOS TOTAL: _____ /4

NOW, PASS THE BOOK TO JESTER 2 →

Jokes

What do you call a cat working in an ambulance?

A PURR-amedic!

_____ /1

What is a dog's favorite meal?

BARK-fest! (Breakfast)

_____ /1

Why did the clock get detention?

For TOCK-ing too much in class.

_____ /1

Why couldn't the horse braid her mane?

She only knew how to do ponytails!

_____ /1

JOKES TOTAL: _____ /4

JESTER 2 CONTINUE TO THE NEXT PAGE ➜

Silly Scenarios

(Act it out!)

Act like a dizzy baby trying to walk. Pretend to fall over and try again!

_____ /2

You are popcorn in the microwave. Starting in a crouched position close to the floor, take a leap into the air and show us how you pop, pop, POP!

_____ /2

SILLY SCENARIOS TOTAL: _____ /4

TiME TO SCORE YOUR POiNTS! ➜

JESTER 1

/8
ROUND TOTAL

JESTER 2

/8
ROUND TOTAL

ROUND CHAMPION

ROUND

8

Jokes

Why did the bread need an air conditioner?

It was feeling a little toasty!

/1

What's hotter than the sun?

The sun times infinity!

/1

What is the rain cloud's favorite ice cream topping?

Sprinkles!

/1

Why are dalmatians so bad at hiding?

They are so easy to SPOT!

/1

JOKES TOTAL: _____ /4

JESTER 1 CONTINUE TO THE NEXT PAGE ➞

Silly Scenarios

(Act it out!)

Act like a scared owl at night. Every sound you hear grabs your attention, then make your eyes **REALLY** big, and give out a scared little "Hoo!"

/2

Act like a lizard that is running over hot rocks. Remember, the faster you go, the less it hurts!

/2

SILLY SCENARIOS TOTAL: _____ /4

NOW, PASS THE BOOK TO JESTER 2 ➡

Jokes

What reindeer never says "Thank you"?

RUDE-olf!

/1

What's a snake's favorite drink?

Coca-Cobra! (Coca-Cola)

/1

What does a bee say when she gets into the hive?

"Hey, honey!"

/1

Why did the train keep switching tracks?

It couldn't CHOO-CHOOse!

/1

JOKES TOTAL: _____ /4

Silly Scenarios

(Act it out!)

Act like a hyper kitten that is trying to catch a laser.

_____ /2

Act like a squeaky little mouse running around the house while searching for cheese. Don't forget to make little squeaks every now and then!

_____ /2

SILLY SCENARIOS TOTAL: _____ /4

TIME TO SCORE YOUR POINTS! →

JESTER 1

/8

ROUND TOTAL

JESTER 2

/8

ROUND TOTAL

ROUND CHAMPION

ROUND

9

Jokes

What kind of stick helps you catch a dolphin?

A fish stick!

/1

Which bear got in trouble for having an attitude?

The Pan-DUH.

/1

Knock knock.
Who's there?
Yaw.
Yaw, who?
Well, you're excited to see me!

/1

What pirate is known for chewing loudly?

/1

Captain Crunch!

JOKES TOTAL: _____ /4

JESTER 1 CONTINUE TO THE NEXT PAGE →

Silly Scenarios

(Act it out!)

Be a snake. Slither around on the ground and hiss at other people if they get too close or laugh at you!

/2

You're the best musician in the world, you can even play food like an instrument! Start eating a meal and then suddenly play your food musically!

/2

SILLY SCENARIOS TOTAL: _____ /4

NOW, PASS THE BOOK TO JESTER 2 ➡

Jokes

What do you call a dog who never stops traveling?

Rover!

/1

What do you call a kangaroo with a feather boa?

A Showy Joey!

/1

When was the duck in a band?

Quack in the day!

/1

Where do cows go to ride rollercoasters?

The A-MOO-sement Park.

/1

JOKES TOTAL: _____ /4

Silly Scenarios

(Act it out!)

Do your best impression of a hula-hooping dog that is exhausted and panting happily!

/2

Grab your invisible surfboard, swim into the ocean and surf the big waves. Don't forget to yell, "Kowabunga!"

/2

SILLY SCENARIOS TOTAL: _____ /4

TIME TO SCORE YOUR POINTS! ➞

JESTER 1

/8

ROUND TOTAL

JESTER 2

/8

ROUND TOTAL

ROUND CHAMPION

ROUND

10

Jokes

What did the light switch say, when the lights went out?

"It's my day OFF!"

_____ /1

What's Goofy's favorite planet?

Pluto, of course!

_____ /1

What do you call it when a pig uses a knife?

Pork Chop!

_____ /1

What is a ninja's favorite drink?

Fruit Punch!

_____ /1

JOKES TOTAL: _____ /4

JESTER 1 CONTINUE TO THE NEXT PAGE

Silly Scenarios

(Act it out!)

While eating dinner, your dog is laying next to you. Pretend to sneak the dog some food and whisper, "Good boy!" before anyone sees!

_____ /2

You are an ant crawling along the floor, trying to avoid the giant steps all around you!

_____ /2

SILLY SCENARIOS TOTAL: _____ /4

STOP NOW, PASS THE BOOK TO JESTER 2 ➡

Jokes

What does a zombie do for fun?

Play dead.

_/1

How does a mermaid buy things?

Sand dollars!

_/1

What kind of reptile can keep a beat?

A Snapping Turtle!

_/1

Who is the dad of the corn family?

Pop-Corn.

_/1

JOKES TOTAL: _/4

Silly Scenarios

(Act it out!)

Be a frustrated bird that can't fly no matter how much you jump and flap your wings. (Don't forget to use your bird noises!)

_____ /2

You are a bullfrog leaping from leaf pad to leaf pad in your home pond. How big are your leaps?! Show everyone!

_____ /2

SILLY SCENARIOS TOTAL: _____ /4

TIME TO SCORE YOUR POINTS! ➜

JESTER 1

/8

ROUND TOTAL

JESTER 2

/8

ROUND TOTAL

ROUND CHAMPION

ADD UP ALL YOUR POINTS FROM EACH ROUND.
THE PLAYER WITH THE MOST POINTS IS CROWNED
THE ULTIMATE LAUGH MASTER!

IN THE EVENT OF A TIE, CONTINUE TO THE ROUND
11 FOR THE TIE-BREAKER ROUND!

JESTER 1 _____
GRAND TOTAL

JESTER 2 _____
GRAND TOTAL

_____

THE ULTIMATE
DON'T LAUGH CHALLENGE MASTER

ROUND 11

11

TIE-BREAKER

(WINNER TAKES ALL!)

Jokes

How do fish like to doodle their names?

With bubble letters!

/1

Where do bugs read their books?

The FLY-brary!

/1

What do you call a hairy couch?

FUR-niture!

/1

What did the skunk say after failing the exam?

"It stunk!"

/1

JOKES TOTAL: ___/4

Silly Scenarios

(Act it out!)

Act like a 1,000-year-old dragon, blowing out your birthday cake. There's a lot of candles so you may need to use your wings, too!

/2

You're a lion who loves to hop like a frog, while roaring loudly to scare the other animals!

/2

SILLY SCENARIOS TOTAL: /4

NOW, PASS THE BOOK TO JESTER 2 ➡

75

Jokes

How do dogs stop a movie?

They press PAWS!

/1

What does a horse say when it walks into the stable?

"Hayyyy!"

/1

Why did the nose dance so well?

He had the BOOGIE in him!

/1

How do you know when a duck farts?

The bubbles...

/1

JOKES TOTAL: _____ /4

Silly Scenarios

(Act it out!)

JESTER 2

You are the most magical fairy/wizard EVER! Use your finger as a wand and be majestic as you cast your spells!

/2 ______

Act like a happy penguin that is cheerleading! Don't forget to dance and sing!

/2 ______

SILLY SCENARIOS TOTAL: ______ /4

TIME TO SCORE YOUR POINTS! →

ADD UP ALL YOUR POINTS FROM THE PREVIOUS ROUND. THE JESTER WITH THE MOST POINTS IS CROWNED THE ULTIMATE DON'T LAUGH CHALLENGE MASTER!

JESTER 1

/8

_____

GRAND TOTAL

JESTER 2

/8

_____

GRAND TOTAL

_____

THE ULTIMATE
DON'T LAUGH CHALLENGE MASTER

Check out our

Visit us at

www.DontLaughChallenge.com

to check out our newest books!

other joke books!

If you have enjoyed our book, we would love for you to review us on Amazon!

Made in the USA
Columbia, SC
17 December 2019

85221839R00046